Snuff Box Theatre in association with Sphinx Theatre present

The World Premiere of

BLUSH

by Charlotte Josephine

First performance at Underbelly, Big Belly at the Edinburgh
Festival Fringe, 6 August 2016.

BLUSH

by Charlotte Josephine

Cast

Woman One	**Charlotte Josephine**
Woman Two	
Woman Three	
Man One	**Daniel Foxsmith**
Man Two	

Creative Team

Director	**Edward Stambollouian**
Designer	**James Turner**
Lighting Designer	**Seth Rook Williams**
Sound Designer	**Harry Blake**
Costume Designer	**Holly Rose Henshaw**
Movement Director	**Polly Bennett**
Script Development	**Sarah Dickenson**
Producer	**Jake Orr**
Production Manager	**Kevin Millband**
PR	**Chloe Nelkin Consulting**

CHARLIE JOSEPHINE
ACTOR AND WRITER

Charlie Josephine is an actor represented by Hatton McEwan Penford and a playwright represented by The Agency. Graduate of the Contemporary Theatre Course, East 15 Acting School, Charlie's first play *Perffection* won a NSDF commendation for writing. *Bitch Boxer* won the Soho Theatre Young Writers Award 2012, Old Vic New Voices Edinburgh Season 2012, British Council Showcase 2013, Holden Street Theatre's Award 2013, Clonmel Theatre Award 2014 and Adelaide Fringe Award 2014. *Bitch Boxer* is published by Methuen Drama and performed internationally. *Blush* won the Underbelly Untapped Edinburgh Season 2016 and The Stage Edinburgh Award 2016. *Pops* won the HighTide Disruption Festival Edinburgh Season 2019 and The Stage Edinburgh Award 2019. *Pops* is published by Methuen Drama. Charlie's audio drama *Massive* is available at Audible, and their play *Birds And Bees* is available as part of a digital package at Theatre Centre. For screen work, Charlie won the inaugural BBC Screenplay First Award, and in March 2017 was named on the BBC New Talent Hotlist. Other acting experience includes *Secret Theatre Company* (Lyric Hammersmith); Phyllida Lloyd's *Julius Caesar* (Donmar Warehouse) and Erica Whyman's *Romeo and Juliet* (RSC).

DANIEL FOXSMITH
PERFORMER

Daniel Foxsmith is an actor and playwright and trained at East 15 Acting School. Selected credits include: *Nothing* (Royal Exhange); *Licensed to Ill* (Southwark Playhouse); *If I Were Me* (Soho Theatre/The Bush); *Enduring Song* (Southwark Playhouse); *The Extraordinary Adventures of Mr Benn* (The Northcott Theatre); *Room on The Broom* (Lyric Theatre, West End); *The Gruffalo* (National Tour/Hong Kong, Manila) and *Bound* (Southwark Playhouse/Adelaide, AUS).

Daniel won Best Performer at The Adelaide Fringe as part of *Bound*, which won a Scotsman Fringe First at the Edinburgh Festival Fringe 2010.

His first play, *The Observatory*, won the Scottish Daily Mail and Conference of Drama Schools Edinburgh Award and National Student Drama Festival and Methuen Drama Prize. His latest play, *Weald*, was shortlisted for the Yale Drama Series Prize 2015, and the inaugural Hodgkiss Award at the Royal Exchange Theatre, and is published by Oberon Books.

Daniel is co-Artistic Director of Snuff Box Theatre along with Charlotte and Bryony Shanahan.

EDWARD STAMBOLLOUIAN
DIRECTOR

Ed trained at the University of Manchester, and went on to an MA in Theatre Directing at Bristol Old Vic Theatre School. Ed was Associate Director to Jamie Lloyd on the West End Trafalgar Transformed Season: *The Pride, The Hothouse* and *Macbeth*. He has also recently worked on education and community projects for The Old Vic, RSC and the National Theatre.

Directing includes: *BLUSH* (New Diorama, then Underbelly, Edinburgh); *Prince of the River* (part of The Old Vic Twelve at Criterion Theatre); *Don't Waste Your Bullets on the Dead* (VAULT Festival); *Invisible Dot Ltd Birthday Bash* (Hammersmith Apollo); *Dan & Phil: The Amazing Tour is Not on Fire* (UK Tour & London Palladium & US/Australian/Europe Tour); *That's The Way Aha Aha Joe Lycett* (Edinburgh Festival & National Tour); *Feathers in the Snow* (The Unicorn Theatre); *Awkward Conversations with Animals I've F*cked* (Underbelly, Edinburgh); *Wedding* (Shoreditch Town Hall & Forest Fringe); *Blacktop Sky*, rehearsed reading (Talawa Studio); *I Started a Fire* (Arcola); *The Pride*, UK Tour (ATG Venues); *Against the Law* (Trafalgar Studios 1); *Family Voices & Victoria Station* (Trafalgar Studios 1); *Outlying Islands*, rehearsed reading (Trafalgar Studios 1); *Knives in Hens*, rehearsed reading (Trafalgar Studios 1); *Gargarin Way*, rehearsed reading (Trafalgar Studios 1); *Joe Lycett: Some Lycett Hot* (Pleasance Courtyard, Edinburgh); *Sure Thing* (Cockpit Theatre); *Finer Noble Gases/Lobby Hero* (Theatre Royal Haymarket); *Every Bit of My Love* (Old Vic Tunnels); *Zombie Nation, 24 Hour Plays* (Old Vic); *The Aliens* (Trafalgar Studios 2); *The Hothouse* (John Thaw Studio, Manchester); *Animal Farm* (John Thaw Studio, Manchester); *The Bacchae* (John Thaw Studio, Manchester) and *Elegy* (Shunt Vaults).

Assistant, Resident & Associate Directing includes: *The Pride* (Trafalgar Studios 1); *The Hothouse* (Trafalgar Studios 1); *Macbeth* (Trafalgar Studios 1); *The Merry Wives of Windsor* (RSC, Stratford-upon-Avon); *School for Scandal* (Theatre Royal, Bath); *Mercury Fur* (Trafalgar Studios); *Honk Honk You Donkey Donk* (Old Vic); *The Lion in Winter* (Theatre Royal Haymarket); *On The Piste* (Tobacco Factory, Bristol); *Richard II* (Tobacco Factory, Bristol); *Aladdin* (Salisbury Playhouse) and *Shoreditch Ball Park* (LIFT, Shoreditch Festival).

Television includes: *BONCAS: British Online Creator Awards* (London Palladium and Online); *Joe Lycett: Live at the Apollo* (BBC One, Apollo Theatre) and *JUNK*, panel show pilot (BBC).

JAMES TURNER
DESIGNER

James trained on the Motley Theatre Design Course. He won the 2013 OffWestEnd Award for Best Set Designer for *Mercury Fur*.

Designs include: *Before The Party* (Salisbury Playhouse); *Home Truths* (Cardboard Citizens); *Dan and Phil: The Amazing Tour is Not on Fire* (World Tour); *Educating Rita* (Hull Truck); *Toast* (UK Tour/59E59, New York/Park Theatre); *A Further Education, State Red* (Hampstead Theatre); *Brenda* (HighTide Festival/ The Yard); *When We Were Women, Buckets* (Orange Tree); *Chicken* (Eastern Angles); *The Deep Blue Sea* (Watermill); *Cuddles* (59E59, New York/Ovalhouse/UK Tour); *The Father* (Trafalgar Studios 2); *Donkey Heart* (Trafalgar Studios 2/Old Red Lion); *The Cherry Orchard Parallel Production* (Young Vic); *Honest* (Salisbury Playhouse/UK Tour); *John Ferguson, A Life, The Sluts of Sutton Drive* (Finborough); *Mercury Fur* (Trafalgar Studios 2/Old Red Lion); *The Hotel Plays* (Langham Hotel); *Our Ajax, I Am A Camera, Execution of Justice* (Southwark Playhouse); *MilkMilkLemonade* (Oval House); *Clybourne Park, In Arabia We'd All Be Kings* (RADA); *Dracula, A Midsummer Night's Dream* (LAMDA); *The Suicide, Cause Célèbre* (CSSD); *Goodnight Children Everywhere* (Drama Centre London); *Thrill Me* (Charing Cross Theatre/Edinburgh Festival/UK Tour) and *Plain Jane* (Royal Exchange Studio).

Work as Associate Designer includes: *Rome Season* (Royal Shakespeare Company); *A View from the Bridge* (Young Vic/ Wyndham's) and *Antigone* (Barbican).

SETH ROOK WILLIAMS
LIGHTING DESIGNER

Seth studied Lighting Design at Wimbledon College of Art and works as a lighting designer in theatre and dance. He is currently working regularly with companies such as Rough Haired Pointer, Igor and Moreno, Gameshow and Nora. Some of his recent designs include: *trade* (Young Vic, Clare); *Weald* (Finborough Theatre); *Operation Crucible* (Sheffield Crudible, Finborough Theatre & National Tour); *Bitch Boxer, Hiraeth,* and *If I Were Me* (Edinburgh Fringe, Soho Theatre & National Tours); *Dancing Bear, Dancing Bear* (National Tour); *Noonday Demons, Christie In Love,* and *Diary of a Nobody* (King's Head Theatre); *The Ingenious Gentleman Don Quixote of la Mancha* (Edinburgh Fringe & European Tour); *Idiot-Syncrasy,* and *A Room For All Our Tomorrows* (International Tours) and *Nora Invites* (Sadlers Wells Studio, European Tour).

HARRY BLAKE
SOUND DESIGNER

Credits include: *The Graduate* (West Yorkshire Playhouse, Leicester Curve and National Tour); *The Snow Child* (Sheffield Crucible); *The Island Nation* (Arcola); *Jason and the Argonauts* (Unicorn); *Night Must Fall* (National Tour); *To Dream Again* (Theatre Clwyd); *Hedda Gabler* (Salisbury Playhouse); *P'yongyang* (Finborough); *Cyrano* (BBC Radio Four); *Bike* (Salisbury Playhouse); *The Future for Beginners* (Wales Millennium Centre and touring); *The Glass Supper* (Hampstead Theatre); *Once upon a Christmas* (Look Left, Look Right); *The Love Girl and the Innocent* (Southwark Playhouse); *Perle* (Tobacco Factory and Soho Theatre); *A Midsummer Night's Dream, Othello* and *Cyrano de Bergerac* (Grosvenor Park Open Air Theatre) *Mobile Phone Show* (Lyric Hammersmith); *The Wind in the Willows* (The Lord Chamberlain's Men); *Twelfth Night* and *Masters, are you mad?* (Grosvenor Park); *MANGA SISTER* (liveartshow@The Yard); *live electronic score for Don Giovanni* (Soho Theatre); *Anna Karenina* (Arcola) and *Monkey and Bear* (InTransit Festival).

Harry is currently Cameron Mackintosh Resident Composer at West Yorkshire Playhouse. He was the first composer appointed to the OLD VIC 12 and is winner of both the Craig Barbour Award for Composition (Soho Theatre) and the Musical Theatre Network Award (2014). He was recently made an associate of the Royal Academy of Music (ARAM) and is one half of the award-winning cabaret act HOUSE OF BLAKEWELL.

HOLLY ROSE HENSHAW
COSTUME DESIGNER

Holly trained at the Royal Central School of Speech and Drama.

Her recent theatre credits include: *French Without Tears* (Orange Tree Theatre & English Touring Theatre); *The Brink, When We Were Women* (Orange Tree Theatre); *Octagon* (Arcola Theatre); *Luce* (Southwark Playhouse); *Dan & Phil: The Amazing Tour Is Not On Fire* (USA & UK Tours); *The One That Got Away* (Bath Theatre Royal); *Forget Me Not* (Bush Theatre); *Handbagged* (Tour 2015); *The Suicide* (Embassy Theatre); *House of Mirrors* and *Hearts* (Arcola Theatre); *Marriage of Figaro* and *Lucia Di Lammermoor* (Diva Opera – European Tour); *The Father* (Trafalgar Studios); *Alligators, The Meeting, The Argument, A Further Education, Sunspots, Deluge, Deposit, Elephants, The Wasp* and *State Red* (Hampstead Theatre); *The Armour* (Defibrillator at the Langham Hotel);

Donkey Heart (Trafalgar Studios); *Goodnight Children Everywhere* (Drama Centre); *Don Giovanni* and *Tales Hoffman* (Diva Opera European Tour).

Holly is an associate designer for Snapdragon Productions and her extensive work for the company includes: *Toast* (59 East 59 New York, UK Tour & Park Theatre); *Teddy* (Southwark Playhouse); *The Dead Wait, Thark* (Park Theatre) and *A Life* (Finborough Theatre).

POLLY BENNETT
MOVEMENT DIRECTOR

Polly Bennett is a Movement Director and Choreographer working nationally and internationally. She holds an MA in Movement from the Royal Central School of Speech and Drama and is Associate Movement Practitioner at the Royal Shakespeare Company.

Theatre credits include: *Woyzeck* (Old Vic Theatre); *Salome* (RSC); *Don Juan in Soho* (Wyndhams); *My Country: A Work in Progress* (National Theatre); *Junkyard* (Bristol Old Vic, Theatre Clywd and Rose Kingston); *Henry V* (RSC/Shanghai Dramatic Arts Centre); *A Streetcar Named Desire* (Royal Exchange); *Blush* (Underbelly); *Travesties* (Menier Chocolate Factory and West End); *The Deep Blue Sea* (National Theatre); *People, Places and Things* (National and West End); *A Midsummer Night's Dream* (RSC); *Doctor Faustus* (Duke of York's); *The Maids* (Trafalgar Studios); *Yen* (Royal Court); *The Lion, the Witch and the Wardrobe* (Birmingham Rep); *Plaques and Tangles* (Royal Court); *Three Days in the Country, Nut* (National Theatre); *Hang* (Royal Court); *The Famous Victories of Henry V* (RSC/UK Tour); *The Rise and Fall of Little Voice* (Birmingham REP/West Yorkshire Playhouse); *The Angry Brigade* (Bush Theatre/Paines Plough); *Pan Oedd Y Byd Yn Fach* (Theatr Genedlaethol Cymru); *A Mad World My Masters* (RSC/UK Tour); *Dunsinane* (National Theatre Scotland/ US, Asia and UK Tour); *Helver's Night* (York Theatre Royal); *Pomona* (Orange Tree Theatre); *The King's Speech* (Chichester/Birmingham REP/UK Tour); *The Kingmaker* (St James Theatre); *Come Fly With Me* (Salisbury Playhouse); *Cinderella and the Beanstalk* (Theatre503); *To Kill a Mockingbird* (Regents Park); *Hopelessly Devoted* (Paines Plough); *Ragnarok* (Eastern Angles); *Mock Tudor* (Pleasance/Theatre503); *Hysteria* (Hampstead Theatre); *Acis and Galatea* (Iford Opera); *Lobsters* (Peep); *Mudlarks* (Bush Theatre); *Celebrity Night at Cafe Red* (Trafalgar Studios) and *Don Juan Comes Back From the War* (Finborough Theatre.)

Other work includes: *Gareth Malone's Best Of British* (BBC);
Fazer's Urban Symphony (Royal Albert Hall/BBC); *The Queen's
Coronation Concerts* (Buckingham Palace/BBC) and *Festival
Of Neighbourhood* (Southbank Centre). Polly was Assistant
Movement Director on the London 2012 Olympic Opening
Ceremony. She was Mass Choreography Assistant on the
London 2012 Olympic Closing Ceremony and Paralympic
Opening Ceremony, and Mass Cast Choreographer on the 2014
Sochi Winter Olympics and Paralympic Opening Ceremonies.

SARAH DICKENSON
SCRIPT DEVELOPMENT

Sarah's roles include: Associate Dramaturg for LAMDA,
Associate Dramaturg for the RSC, Production Dramaturg for
the Globe, Senior Reader at Soho Theatre, Literary Manager
from Theatre503, New Writing Associate at The Red Room and
founding Coordinator for the South West New Writing Network.
She has worked on performance projects and artistic development
nationally and internationally for a wide range of organisations and
theatre makers including Theatre Centre, Y Labordy, writernet,
National Theatre, Hampstead Theatre, Kaleider, The Wrong
Crowd, Bristol Old Vic, Theatre Bristol, Old Vic New Voices,
Liverpool Everyman, Champloo, Ustinov Bath, Plymouth Theatre
Royal, Tamasha, Apples and Snakes, The Almeida, Hall for
Cornwall, The Fence and Churchill Theatre Bromley.

JAKE ORR
PRODUCER

Jake is a freelance producer and programmer. He is producer
for Snuff Box Theatre and is Artistic Director and Founder of
A Younger Theatre. Jake co-directs and produces the annual
Incoming Festival. Jake is also co-Director of producing
company Making Room working with artists across the UK.
As an independent producer he has produced *BLUSH* (Snuff
Box Theatre at Edinburgh Fringe Festival, Soho and on Tour);
Weald (Snuff Box Theatre and Finborough Theatre) and *Shelter
me* (Theatre Delicatessen). As Associate Producer his credits
include: *The Bombing of the Grand Hotel* (Cockpit Theatre
and Tour); *Mouse Plague* (Edinburgh Festival Fringe, BAC
and Tour) and *The Eradication of Schizophrenia in Western
Lapland* (Edinburgh Festival Fringe, BAC and Tour). Jake also
co-curates *Dialogue with Maddy Costa* and produces Dialogue
Festival. He was a freelance marketer before moving into
producing and is a trustee of Boundless Theatre. Jake was
nominated as Best Producer in the 2014 OffWestEnd Awards.

SNUFF BOX THEATRE

Snuff Box Theatre is a multi-award winning collective formed in 2011 by Bryony Shanahan, Charlotte Josephine and Daniel Foxsmith. The company has produced four shows to date including *Weald*, *Bitch Boxer*, *The Altitude Brothers* and *The Observatory*. *Weald* was shortlisted for the Hodgkiss Award and the Yale Drama Series Prize and included a nomination for Best Actor in the OffWestEnd Awards. *Bitch Boxer* won the Soho Theatre Young Writers Award, Old Vic New Voices Edinburgh and the Adelaide Fringe Award before touring nationally and internationally. *The Observatory* won the Ideastap/NSDF/Methuen Edinburgh Award and the Scottish Daily Mail/CDS Edinburgh Drama Award.

www.snuffboxtheatre.co.uk | @SnuffBoxTheatre #BLUSHplay | facebook.com/SB.Theatre

With thanks to...

Camden People's Theatre, New Diorama Theatre, Sphinx Theatre, the Unity Theatre Trust and the Peggy Ramsay Foundation. Bryony Shanahan. Sarah Dickenson. Simon Stephens and Sean Holmes. Uri Roodner. Matt Burman. Michael Smiley. Lily Einhorn. Jon Foster, Holly Augustine and Suzanne Crothers. Sumera Syed and Kara Messina. Dr Brene Brown and Elizabeth Gilbert. Dame Harriet Walter, Peggy Ramsay and all of our generous Kickstarter backers: Chris Snow, Sebastian Tirant, Catherine Major, Ben Whybrow, Jenny Whybrow, Adam El-Hagar, Jon Foster, Kate Hatton, David Kirk, Aidan McGlynn, Jonathan, Malcolm Heyhoe, Eleanor Turney, Kirsty Connell, Julia Haworth, Rania Jumaily, Adam Bacon, Simon Maeder, Tid, Maria Ferguson, Ian, Rob Hadley, Libby and Nev Thomas, Adam Morley, Zoe Cooper, Amanda Dalton, Eve Hedderwick Turner, OpenWorks Theatre, Flavia Fraser-Cannon, Jack Lynch, Stanley Walton, Heidi Brown, Allan Wilson, Nicola Coughlan, Merce Ribot, Holly Augustine and Charlie Parker. Further thanks to Mike Gilhooly, Theatre N16, Christopher Hone, Kit Nairne and Making Room.

Note – For information on requesting performance rights please contact The Agency on info@theagency.co.uk or +44 (0)20 77271346.

Photo credit: The Other Richard

BLUSH

Charlotte Josephine

BLUSH

methuen | drama

LONDON • NEW YORK • OXFORD • NEW DELHI • SYDNEY

METHUEN DRAMA
Bloomsbury Publishing Plc
50 Bedford Square, London, WC1B 3DP, UK
1385 Broadway, New York, NY 10018, USA
29 Earlsfort Terrace, Dublin 2, Ireland

BLOOMSBURY, METHUEN DRAMA and the Methuen Drama logo are
trademarks of Bloomsbury Publishing Plc

First published in Great Britain by Oberon Books 2017
This edition published by Methuen Drama 2021

Cover design: Daniel Foxsmith
Cover image: The Other Richard

A catalogue record for this book is available from the British Library.

ISBN: PB: 978-1-3502-6276-8
eBook: 978-1-7868-2016-7

To find out more about our authors and books visit www.bloomsbury.com
and sign up for our newsletters.

Note: */.. indicates where a word can't be found, and a sound or gesture is used to articulate something instead.*

A two-hander, performed by one actress and one actor. The performers multi-role, swapping character and gender easily. To begin there's a moment of movement, or stillness, where we see the actors and they see us. The actors check in with each other, seeing if they're ready to begin. Then the actress steps forward to play WOMAN ONE and directly addresses the audience.

WOMAN ONE: I'd like to take out each and every one of their eyeballs. Pluck them out, ever so gently and easily, with a precision and a grace that suggests I've done this a thousand times before. And by the end I will have, I'll have done it thirty thousand times. I'd like to place them, ever so gently, on the floor in neat little rows, all lined up next to each other like soldiers. I'd like to stand back and admire them, just for a moment. The light shining off the cornea, fluid around the pupils gleaming like oyster pearls, like spilt egg yoke, like smokers spit on concrete. I'd like to admire them, thirty thousand pairs, strange in their beauty. An image I know will be branded tonight on the inside of my lids when I close my eyes to sleep. It's calming, looking at them sat patiently in their neat little lines, it's pleasing somehow, the regimented lines, the order, clinical and neat, it's pleasing to look at, somehow the precision is comforting.

I'd like to remove my shoes. And then I'd like to remove my socks. I want to be barefoot. It's *important* that I am barefoot, that my feet are, naked, that my skin can feel. The floor would be cold and that would, like the regimented lines, be somewhat somehow pleasing. I'm *pleased* the floor is cold, the temperature is correct somehow, it's comforting.

I would like to take a step, barefoot, towards the first pair of eyes. I would like to, slowly, without slipping off them, or knocking them out of line, I would like to slowly, stand on each one of those eyeballs. Stand on them barefoot. I want to be barefoot so I can feel each one strain under my weight, feel each one bulge under the arch of my foot as I apply more pressure, more weight, more of me, until the sweet surrender of it's explosion under the skin of my foot. It's pop into non-existence squishing between my toes and oozing across the cold floor that's temperature is somehow comforting, the sound of each one popping is somehow comforting, thirty thousand pairs popped and I would somehow be comforted, and revenge would be had, and closure would be found, and peace would be restored and that, that is what I would like. *Very much.*

Thirty thousand. The number of views on the website. Thirty thousand, in what, twenty-four hours? My sister's only just eighteen. He was her first boyfriend, she trusted him, he thought it'd be funny. I want to smash his face in, I want to smash his face until there is nothing but bits of bloody bone, I've never felt such a terrible, fucking, *rage.* She says she feels like she's been raped. She says she feels like she's been raped thirty thousand times. She's just eighteen.

MAN TWO: Women round here seem to want a big handbag and a boyfriend with big arms. I'm in a pub, south of the river. We've had a team-building day off-site. Team bollocks day, waste of time. We've all sacked it off early, hit the nearest pub. Looks like every other pub these days, all cream and green and brown. Blackboard with chalk, candles. Steve's talking and we're pretending to listen because technically he's our superior, but basically he's a cunt. Thing is, he might be the big-wig at work because he's bouncing on a bigger wage packet and a sharper suit and a faster car. But here, in this pub, he's nothing. Because here in this pub, he's quite clearly physically less imposing than the hench fuckers full of stella crowding round the bar. They know it and he knows it. It's a hierarchy that shifts determined on your surroundings. So he talks louder, using longer words to try and sound clever, and we all laugh at his jokes that aren't funny. I down my pint, announce I'm going for a piss and get about thirty seconds of peace before he bangs the door open after me. And that's when it happens, I have an epiphany. About cocks. About the size of cocks.

You see, no matter how much people bang on that the
best things in life are free this city's still fucking expensive.
It's a dog eat dog world and I want to provide for my
family. And yeah, I want to look good whilst I'm doing
that. People say it's an inside job but bollocks, everyone's
looking at the outside stuff. The job, the house, the car, the
wife, the kids, the holiday. None of that matters if you're
hung like a newborn baby in the artic. Having a small cock
cuts across all of that. It's primal. Caveman. God given,
or not given, as the case may be. And here in this urinal,
pissing on those little yellow cubes trying to make them
move without splashing on my jeans I spot it. Just a glance.
I'm not gay. I catch a glimpse and it changes everything.
It explains why he's so up tight, why he's so/.. I watch
him at the bar get annoyed when she pours the wrong
lager and I know. I watch him moan about Susan getting
the promotion we all applied for and I know. I watch him
watching the girls at the end of the bar, watch him slurp his
pint and swallow hard, watch his eyes fixed on them over
his glass, *and I know*. And if he says he's fine with that, then
he's a fucking liar.

WOMAN THREE: I squeeze myself, deliberately, between
two people every time I'm on the tube. Even though the
carriage is empty further down I squeeze in, like this,
between strangers. Push my shoulders back to slot between
them, ignoring subtle shoves of disapproval. Little angry
rearrangement of bags and coats until finally we're settled.
All squished up like sardines. Their arms on my arms,
pining me in on either side I lean back in the seat and
breathe, in time with them.

And it feels good. Because, I know this sounds mad but,
it's been a while since I've been touched, by anyone. And I
don't mean it, *like that*, I mean literally no one has touched
me, for days now. It can be like that in London sometimes,
can't it? It's a lonely city? And *I don't know*, I can't
remember what it feels like, what my skin feels like, where
my edges are and, I know it's sad and mad and/.. But I'm
starting to wonder if I'm fading somehow? Impossible but,

becoming invisible? I see everyone floating around, being busy, doing life, and *I don't know*. It makes things normal, makes me feel, held. Propped up my two strangers stops the empty spilling out of my ribs and for just a little while we're all moving along together, in the same direction, and it feels ok.

MAN ONE: Business class is the bollocks! One TEDTalk and suddenly all this?! The Internet is a strange beast. *We would like to invite you to speak at this years Bright Young Minds conference held in,* New York City baby! I mean?! Part of me still thinks it's an administrative error, and they'll send me packing soon as I arrive. Look, press that one and the seat moves, nice eh?

I'm wearing my lucky socks. I know, I know! But my sister made me. She said, '*I'm really proud of yer, wear your socks, don't fuck it up!*' She's ace. I mean, bloomin' 'eck! Things like this don't happen to blokes like me. I'm usually *behind* the screen, not *on* it! Not talking to thousands of people, not *me!* And yet, here we are?! New haircut, new suit, lucky socks, upgraded to business class, and it is dead classy. I could get used to this!

I can't stop looking at that couple sat across the aisle. They're 'bout the same age as me I reckon, but proper glossy. He's all action-man-arms in a Fred Perry shirt and she's so pretty it hurts. But it's like he's bloody forgot who he's sat next to, daft sod, cus he's ignoring her and playing on his iPad? Some stupid game that I think's one of ours. And she's stuck to her phone, manicured hands clasped round a shiny slick screen. Clicks and swipes, clicks and swipes, throughout this whole flight they ain't look up once, glued. Out the window the sun sinks through marshmallow pink clouds, whoever painted that sky were showing off. But these two are missing it, totally absorbed in a screen lit world like the real one's borin'. He's got three of our logos on his screen, lad's got good taste. And I guess I should probably feel proud but/.. They're sat side by side, click and swipe, click and swipe, and I

want to lean across to tell them it's ok to put those down
you know. I designed most of the stuff you're using and I
really won't be offended if you put it down to, talk to each
other, or look out the window, or whatever. I mean we're
flying! We're thirty six thousand feet up in the air in a little
metal can zooming across the sky. Young love, side-by-
side, a thousand miles apart. We land and I breeze through
customs like a panther in me new suit. Very swish.

ACTRESS: *Ping!*

MAN ONE: Email from Dave.

ACTRESS: *How was the flight?*

MAN ONE: Cheeky sod.

ACTRESS: *P.S. – Enjoy the car.*

MAN ONE: A shiny black BMW is waiting to pick me up,
the driver has got a hat on like this is a fucking film or
something. Suddenly it hits me. I'm in New York! I'm
about to go give a lecture to the world's greatest young
entrepreneurs. I am living the dream. I feel/… Ok *Bright
Young Minds*, let's be 'aving yer.

WOMAN TWO: He sent me a photo of his cock. Fully erect,
his sweaty palm pulling at it, the first bead of semen sat
glistening on the tip. I'm in Sainsbury's buying washing
detergent wondering if I really need non-bio. The bio stuff
is 64p cheaper. Vaguely remember having a rash once,
is that worth 64p?

ACTOR: *Ping!*

WOMAN TWO: It's a text from him.

ACTOR: *'R U Horny?'*

WOMAN TWO: R. U. I hate it when people do that. Missing
letters really grate on me. Reply, *'yes'*, full stop. Though the
answer is obviously no. I'm in Sainsbury's.

The speed of his reply is both astonishing and irritating as
fuck. I mean if I text him about anything, *anything* other
than sex he takes *forever* to reply. I'm left waiting for *days*,
driving myself mad checking my phone a *thousand* times.
Little blue screen's my night-light as I lie awake waiting for
him to love me. Phantom beeps interrupt my sleep, makes

my heart skip a beat then plummet back into the dark fucking depths of disappointment. And here, back here to the present, to Sainsbury's, to cold strip light and cold tile floor, I send a 'yes' and he replies instantly.

ACTOR: *Ping!*

WOMAN TWO: With a photo of his cock. And I stare at it. And then I stare at the non-bio. Cock. Non-bio. Cock. Non-bio. Cock. Non-bio. Cock.

And praps it's 'cus I'm in Sainsbury's? Or praps it's cus I'm over-saturated, and I've become numb to nudity. Praps I'm now suddenly gay? Or praps it's cus it's not a particularly nice image to look at, I mean they ain't never really very pretty, whatever, basically I feel *nothing*. Absolutely nothing. I feel the same way looking at the photo of his cock as I do looking at the non-bio. It's been at least a minute so he texts.

ACTOR: *'Well?...'*

WOMAN TWO: Question mark. Dot. Dot. Dot. And maybe it's 'cus I'm bored? Dot, dot, dot. Maybe I'm hanging onto the idea that romance isn't dead? Dot, dot, dot. And this is modern romance? Dot, dot. Maybe it'll make me feel something? Dot. Anything?

I hold my thumb on the letter 'm''until it fills the screen. And type *'I can't wait'*. I get the bio stuff. Skin might not like it, but it's cheap and a girl's gotta do what a girl's gotta do right?

(Movement – we see the actors again, and they see us. A physical shift into a new dynamic. A score of abstract movement that we'll see the origin of in real time throughout the play.)

WOMAN ONE: Mum's shrunk in shame on the sofa and my sister hasn't left her room in days. Right, I'm going to have to fix this myself, I march down the police station, googling the law on the way. *Sexually explicit images or videos shared without consent with the intent to cause harm.* There, look! It's illegal, why aren't you arresting him?! He doesn't seem to know, just keeps telling me it's,

POLICEMAN: A bit more complicated than that madam.

WOMAN ONE: How is it?! The law's just been passed,
    it's illegal! Everyone's calling her a slut. He's humiliated
    her, arrest him! He shakes his head,

POLICEMAN: He wasn't acting with the specific intent to
    harm. The school told us that he sent the video to just two
    friends, who then in turn passed it on.

WOMAN ONE: Arrest *them*! Someone's put it on websites,
    pornsites!

POLICEMAN: I'm afraid the law currently excludes those
    who share images and videos for their own amusement
    or financial gain.

WOMAN ONE: What?!

POLICEMAN: It's a new law. They're still negotiating.
    These things take/

WOMAN ONE: So they just get away with it?!

POLICEMAN: He's been suspended from school as
    punishment; he's really very sorry for/

WOMAN ONE: I don't give a fuck!

POLICEMAN: Calm down madam.

WOMAN ONE: This is abuse. My sister is being abused.
    Arrest *someone!*

POLICEMAN: Madam, I promise you, we are doing the very
    best that we/

WOMAN ONE: Well it's not good enough!

POLICEMAN: I know.

(Beat.)

I know. This must be horrible for you/

WOMAN ONE: My sister is/

POLICEMAN: I can't imagine how your sister must be feeling.
    What she's been through is horrendous, and you wouldn't
    want to drag that out any further. It's not always so black
    and white. I'm very sorry, but there's really not much else
    we can do.

(WOMAN ONE nods quietly.)

WOMAN THREE: I've got a new phone, upgraded. It's really
    shiny, feels nice in my hand. Makes me feel like one of
    those women you know, all like, *mine's a skinny latte.* It's a
    really good one, it's got all of these, features, on it. But the

best thing about it is the camera, the camera is really good. I've been taking photographs of everything. Taking loads of photos of myself. It's weird because, suddenly it's like, *oh*, is that what I look like? And, *oh*, I actually look, quite pretty in that one. I've changed my profile picture and I've already got seventeen "likes" in five minutes. People are commenting on it.

FACEBOOK: *'Looking good hun!'… 'Wowza!'… 'Gorgeous!'*

WOMAN THREE: I'm going to take more, to see what I look like doing different things. So I can show people me looking good doing different things. I've signed up for all of the social media sites and uploaded a profile, and everyone is saying I look great. And I'm starting to feel great, and this morning I uploaded a dating app, *I know!* And I put all of these pictures of me looking pretty and men have started talking to me, asking me all these questions. And I've started speaking to one of them in particular and he's *really nice*, look. He says he thinks I'm *'really sexy'*, look!

MAN TWO: Friday afternoon school run and I'd rather be in the pub. *Put your belts on girls.* Amy slams the door as Lizzie spills the beans.

LIZZIE: '*Daddy, Amy had sex education today!'*
AMY: *'Shut up Lizzie!'*
LIZZIE: *'Miss Harris says we'll have it when we're older. Is it true I'll bleed in my knickers? The boys were talking about blowjobs, what's a blowjob?'*

MAN TWO: Amy's blush burns through the wing mirror as my heart stops. She hands me some sweaty leaflets and a paper bag of condoms. I mean, Jesus fucking Christ! She's thirteen! She's not/.. What are they playing at?! *Belts on girls.* I want to wrap them up in cotton wool. I want to plug cotton wool deep into their ears, stuff it into their mouths, up their nose, wrap it round their beautiful heads, cover every fucking inch of their precious bodies in cotton wool until nothing or no one can get in.

AMY: *Dad!*

MAN TWO: Fuck, I'm speeding. Traffic lights. Breathe. *Beep beep beep beep beep.* Yummy Mummys with prams like tanks and posh kids from the school we can't afford bumble across the road like they own it. Schoolboys at the bus stop, all glued to their phones. Look in the wing mirror and see Amy on hers. *Fuck.* Pull a U-Turn.

AMY: *Dad what are you doing?!*

MAN TWO: Zoom back up the hill. *Wait here.* Slam the door, march across the playground, crash into the office and scream at the secretary, *they're all watching porn!* Fuck. Breathe. I'm told to take a seat.

WOMAN THREE: I want to be seen, like those women who turn heads you know? I want to feel as good as she looks, all like/.. I've started taking sexier photos, like the girls in magazines, and I sent a few to him.

ACTOR: *Ping!*

WOMAN THREE: Oh my god, he says I'm *'really hot'.*

ACTOR: *Ping!*

WOMAN THREE: He's asked me for naked photos.

MAN TWO: I practice in the corridor. Mr Headmaster, sir. *(Coughs.)* Ok. Sex education in this country is a fucking joke. It's so Victorian. Bare bones biology – here is a penis, here is a vagina. Engage in sexual intercourse you'll get diseases, or pregnant. No talk of joy? Of pleasure? What if you're gay? Pornography provides more sex education than school ever did. British embarrassment, blushing and bumbling over the birds and the bees. Meanwhile young boys are jizzing over girl's faces because porn has taught them that's sexy. And girls are pretending to enjoy being jizzed on because porn has taught them that's empowerment. And no one's taught anyone where the clit is! Maybe I won't say clit.

SECRETARY: Mr Davies?

MAN TWO: Shit.

SECRETARY: The Head's been delayed. You'll be seen as soon as possible.

MAN TWO: Thanks… Breathe. *(Practicing.)* How am I gonna say this? I don't want you teaching her about sex. Well I do, but not like this, not like how I was taught, because I know what's out there.

WOMAN TWO: I watch porn.

(Beat. The ACTOR looks at the ACTRESS.)

ACTRESS: Loads of women do.

(Beat. They turn back out and continue with the script.)

MAN TWO: I watch porn.

WOMAN TWO: I love it. Ain't much in life that a bath and a bash won't fix.

MAN TWO: And look, I'm a liberal bloke, I'd consider myself a feminist.

WOMAN TWO: Dunno why women don't talk about it.

MAN TWO: I'm a leftie.

WOMAN TWO: Why everyone pretends they don't do it.

MAN TWO: I recycle.

WOMAN TWO: Because they fuckin' do.

MAN TWO: Maybe that's not relevant I just mean I'm not a cunt. I know I can be a bit/.. But I'm not an idiot, I'm not nasty. I'm not like those blokes who/.. I just like sex, a lot.

WOMAN TWO: Fuck the stuff though that's just so *obviously* for men. All screamin' gymnastics and bodies like plastic. Nah that don't turn me on at all.

MAN TWO: For us it was magazines.

WOMAN TWO: You can tell when she's fakin' it.

MAN TWO: Sticky pages shared amongst your mates.

WOMAN TWO: The bloke's never fakin' it.

MAN TWO: Sneaking downstairs to watch your dad's VHS.

WOMAN TWO: So many videos yeah, well all of them really let's be honest, they're all from his eyes.

MAN TWO: But now they've got the Internet on their phones.

WOMAN TWO: So after a while I get this, it's mad but, I start thinkin' I'm him. I'm him, fuckin' her.

MAN TWO: And it's twenty-four hours and it's free.

WOMAN TWO: Not like I'm gay, the woman's still me it's/..
I'm not makin' sense.

MAN TWO: An endless supply for the endlessly searching.

WOMAN TWO: It's like I imagine I'm *him too*?

MAN TWO: It's all much more aggressive now.

WOMAN TWO: I'm both *him and her*.

MAN TWO: All hair pulling and hand-around-the-throat kisses.

WOMAN TWO: I'm fuckin' me, gettin' fucked by me.

MAN TWO: Plastic bodies and louder noises.

WOMAN TWO: It's weird.

MAN TWO: All girls want to be waxed. Which is just *weird*,
like they've not grown pupes yet? All blokes want to fuck
up the bum now and I bet they didn't like twenty years ago
or whatever.

WOMAN TWO: And now when I'm actually wiv a bloke and
he's doin' me from behind or whatever, I get this like,
video, in my 'ead.

MAN TWO: Every video is the same, like it's choreographed,
since when did sex get choreographed?

WOMAN TWO: I know what I look like for him yeah. Can see
it from his point of view in my 'ead.

MAN TWO: She poses for him, she sucks his cock, he fucks her
in about five positions.

WOMAN TWO: I know how to arch my back and that. Know
how to how to angle myself so I look good.

MAN TWO: Then he cums on her face. Unless it's 'bi-racial'
then he cums on her arse.

WOMAN TWO: Can get off on the idea of what he sees.

MAN TWO: And if it's 'female friendly', she pretends to enjoy
him shoving his finger up her and giving her a quick lick,
before she sucks his dick for twenty minutes.

WOMAN TWO: I dunno. Sometimes it works.

MAN TWO: It always ends the same, him pounding away
'til the money shot.

WOMAN TWO: I still watch it. 'Course I do.

MAN TWO: And now *my daughter* is/.. And you think a quick
'in-out-in-out-diagram' is going to be enough? Then off she
wanders into a world of men like/.. Men who/.. Because

it's not our fault, I mean you can't really blame us, with it so easy to get. And then yeah, after you do feel a bit bad yeah. Like when you've had McDonalds or something. Porn is like the Maccy-Ds of wanking, Double-Ds Maccy-Ds. Feels so good at the time then after it's like *oh I'm just a fucking scumbag, why did I do that? Why haven't I got a bit more self-control or self-worth or something?* And you exit the site, *click*, and my girls, a photo of my beautiful girls is on my home screen and *oh I'm just fucking awful.*

SECRETARY: Mr Davies?

MAN TWO: Shit.

SECRETARY: You can go through now.

MAN TWO: *Thanks…* Ok, breathe… *Fuck.* The headmaster's a bird?! *I erm, (coughs) the thing is, this whole sex education thing. I erm, I think it's important and erm, yeah. I just want to check that, you know/..* Fuck. Breathe. I'm assured that,

HEADMASTER: The syllabus is in accordance with the government's guidelines.

MAN TWO: It's suggested I,

HEADMASTER: Write a letter to the board of governors if you wish to interrogate the matter further.

MAN TWO: And I'm asked,

HEADMASTER: Is there's anything else?

MAN TWO: *Nah, nah you're alright.* Bollocks.

WOMAN ONE: I can't remember leaving the police station. I'm sat in my car, outside my house, *my* hands are on the steering wheel. So I must have driven here? My phone rings, it's my sister and I/.. I'm sat in my car, outside my house. I remember the officer, I remember his face, his, *it's not always so black and white?* She phones again and I/.. Why can't I remember leaving? How weird?! I can't remember the drive home at *all*, but I'm here so I must've, I must be. She phones again, and I/.. I/.. I just, can't, right now. Not 'til I've sorted it out.

MAN ONE: Backstage and I think I need a piss, I've just been but. Fuck. This is. Fuck. You can see the seats from here, see the lights and. Fuck.

ACTRESS: *Ping!*

MAN ONE: It's my sister!

ACTRESS: *'good luck little bro, don't fall over.'*

MAN ONE: Oh great, now I'm worried 'bout that! Got about
a minute. Ok, ok, you're ok. Ok hello, h-hello *Bright Young
Minds.* Hello thank you, bright young, thank you. Oh fuck.

WOMAN THREE: I'm going to do it, I think I...yeah, yeah
I'm going to do it. Waaaaah! *(She sends a photo.)* Sent...
Oh my god. I know it's wrong but, but it feels *really good.*
Really...*exciting!*

ACTOR: *Ping!*

WOMAN THREE: He likes it, he likes me.

ACTOR: *Ping!*

WOMAN THREE: *(She reads it and laughs.)* He's so funny.

ACTOR: *Ping!*

WOMAN THREE: *(She looks at us, grins and sends another photo.)*
I sent another one. *Argh!* This feels *good!*

ACTOR: *Ping!*

WOMAN THREE: He says he can't wait to meet me! I'm sure
everyone's doing it all the time aren't they? People just
don't talk about it. Everyone does it, even those celebrities
got caught doing it didn't they? This is the modern world
isn't it? It's the way things are done. And it feels *good!*
Hello snap and flash and Instagram filters and likes and
shares and comments. Hello silk thong! Hello tinder!
I don't feel invisible anymore, I can feel my skin again
and I know where my edges are. I am Modern Woman,
I am Beyoncé, I am Aphrodite and it feels *fucking great!*

*(Movement – 'joy dance' – something abstract that captures the
jubilant empowerment WOMAN THREE feels. It's bursting with joy,
it looks like a lot of fun, we want to join in. At some point the ACTOR
stops dancing to read the below MAN ONE lecture.)*

MAN ONE: Thank you *Bright Young Minds,* thank you, it's great
to be here. For those of you that don't know me
I'm co-artistic director for FLEXI CX in Manchester.
My expertise range from Product Development,
Gamification, Information Architecture, Customer

Experience and Interaction Design across all touch-points and devices. In short, I'm an Experience Designer. I explore the connections between humans and the technology we use daily, and I help companies create apps and services, which provide their customers with a specific experience.

Now, advertising that's designed to stimulate the brain is not news. Back in the early 90s the Z.M.E.T studies demonstrated how logos and brand names can elicit the same response in the brain as emotions. I won't bore you brainy bunch with stuff you already know. You mark the new wave of exciting entrepreneurs, your ideas are already knocking down doors and winning awards. But your shiny new app means nothing at all if nobody uses it. *(Beat.)* What I do want to do, today and tomorrow whilst I'm here with you, is provoke the idea that the best designs *reward* attention rather than *demand* it. We can change a customer's relationship with their technological devices by firstly examining their current day. The most successful apps work in sync with a customer's existing daily routine, offering a service or experience that really enhances their world. The effect can be so fluid that in time we'll feel baffled as to how we lived before your invention.

(Music stops.)

WOMAN TWO: Summinks gone wrong. I text him. Twice. And he's not replied, which ain't that unusual, we're both busy people yeah, so I don't think much of it and actually it's a few days later before I even realize I've text him three times. Four. *Five?* Five and no reply?! *Shaaaame!* Why the silence? Send a photo of me in the thong he likes, that'll get his attention.

MAN ONE: Now, at the risk of offending some very smart people in some very white coats, I'll speed you through my neurological research. The Limbic Section is my favorite part of the brain. It's the nightclub of neurotransmissions, the factory that forms our emotions, memories and, most importantly, our habits. Dopamine is the sex, drugs and

18

rock and roll of neurotransmitters. It might also be, for an Experience Designer like myself, a secret weapon.

When humans experience feel-good sensations the central cerebral cortex releases dopamine into the Meso-Limbic pathway. A tiny but important brain tract that connects the Nucleus Accumbens to the frontal lobes. Basically, we are literally genetically programmed to remember things, and if we like them, to repeat them until they become a habit. *It's a simple neurological equation*; if a behavior leads to a good feeling, repeat. The most successful apps in the market are designed to be associated with that equation, that's my job, to design dopamine bombs.

So step one is to make sure your app sets a task, a challenge, so when your customer feels like they've actually achieved something, BOOM, good feelings. Wolfram Schultz taught us that an *unexpected* reward releases more dopamine. The most addictive word in the dictionary is '*maybe*', introduce a '*maybe*' and watch dopamine levels skyrocket. The trick is people, to mix it up, it's the novelty of varying the reward that multiples the effect.

WOMAN TWO: No reply. What the fuck? I phone him. No answer. Phone again. He's blocked my number? He's blocked my fucking, for nothing! For no reason? What the fuck?!

MAN ONE: Step two is engaging with altruism. MRI studies reveal that when we perform an act of kindness our reward center is aroused, altruism is a massive trigger for dopamine. We literally get a kick out of sharing something useful on social media, and we encourage each other to do the same.

WOMAN TWO: And just like that yeah, he disappears. Nah listen, *he disappears.* He's nowhere. Gone. Can't find him on Facebook, Twitter, fuckin' LinkedIn, nowhere. He's ghost me. And I don't know what I did, what did I do wrong? He's/.. *Fuck!* His silence is so fuckin' loud yeah, my ears are ringin'. Nah I'm not being poetic, they're actually ringin', I've been doctors. They said it's nuffink, stress... I'm gonna find him. Find out what the fuck he's playin' at.

MAN ONE: Third and final step is the Zeigarnik Effect. Bluma Zeigarnik discovered our tendency to experience intrusive thoughts about an objective that was once pursued and left incomplete. So it's vital that your projects apply the Z effect. If there's no solid conclusion to your task, no end point to your app, then the Z-Effect keeps us coming back for more and more until we literally can't put it down. Combining these three methods is a failsafe formula, it never fails to ensure predictable, precise and perfect designs.

WOMAN THREE: My flatmate walks into my room and catches me taking photos of myself, and I am so humiliated I want to smash her face shut in the door. *(Beat.)* She moans on and on telling me how dangerous it is, and she hopes I haven't actually sent them to anyone. *No, of course not, I'm not stupid, they're just for me, I'm, I'm experimenting.*

FLATMATE: *Well good, because no one can love you until you love yourself you know.*

WOMAN THREE: *I do love myself actually, I felt invisible before and now I'm, I'm.*

FLATMATE: *I'm just worried about you. And turn the noise off, it's annoying.*

MAN TWO: We get home and the girls are straight away fighting over the TV remote like nothing at all has changed. My wife's in the kitchen cooking, spag bol, again, which is fine it's fine. And I try, fuck, breathe. *(Coughs.) Hi love, so erm, yeah, the weirdest thing happened today and I. I'm not sure, erm. (Coughs.)* Fuck. Breathe. Her eyes streaming onion fumes stare at me, knife in hand, juice dripping down her arm she stares, *what are you talking about?* And I try to stumble through what's happened, try to explain that I couldn't explain that, *I don't know what to do?!* She snaps that she doesn't know what I'm talking about, says she's really busy and really tired and can I just please spit it out whatever it is, because she doesn't have time for this right now, in fact can I please go put the bins out, fix the garage door and empty the dishwasher, thanks.

WOMAN ONE: The alarm rings but I'm already awake, I've hardly slept, policemen and teachers spinning round my head. I'd really like to stay in bed, preferably for the rest of my life, but like most people this morning I've got to go to work. Keep calm and carry on. My sister's text four times in the night but I just/.. I can't, right now. I've got to do a presentation today. I need to be determined, focused, positive.

I put on matching underwear. I know that's ridiculous but I feel like I need battle armor to leave the house and pretend to be a functioning human. Matching underwear feels like the right place to start. A little secret boost, something just for me, to make me feel, something. Clean blouse, expensive skirt, new tights. Put on some makeup, hands shaking a little bit but I manage. Last look in the mirror, well done. I look good, almost pretty from a distance, like I'm ready at least, ready for the day. Leaving the house the sun is shining, it feels good on my skin, and for a moment I've almost forgotten, and that feels, nice.

Up ahead of me is a white van and about five blokes are standing around it. They're in overalls with paint on, their faces are covered in paint and dust. How have they've got so messy so quickly? It's still early. They're drinking cans of coke, and polystyrene cups of tea. They're laughing about something. Stained teeth drip spit as heads crack back and beer guts jiggle over dirty jeans. One of them spots me walking towards them and I immediately feel my stomach clench. I'm not sucking it in, it's done it itself, like a self-protection thing? I really don't want to but I have to keep walking towards them, it's the only way to get to work and besides they've all seen me now. One says,

BUILDER: *'Fucking hell!'*

WOMAN ONE: and they're laughing, and my skin's burning. I am so embarrassed at the idea these men find me attractive, and I am mortified at the idea they don't.

BUILDER: *'Morning darlin''*

WOMAN ONE: And I can't answer my whole body is screaming. Stuck, can't breathe, rabbit in headlights skinned alive their eyes stare red hot my nipples burning hot, my bum cunt stomach hips shame sick. Skin tucks up tight, crawling, hot sick panic. Fat tongue taste metal. Hot, they're eyes burn, their eyes, thirty thousand eyes leave marks on my. Slimy dirty stupid slut. My sister. Click. She's up for it. Click fuckin' bitch. Their eyes burn my thighs, like it's my fault like I wanted? Greedy, angry, hot, horrible fucking horrible want to open my mouth and SCREAM! Please don't please don't please don't please don't please don't please don't one walks deliberately right across my path and I almost trip and someone touches my arm,

BUILDER: '*Oh, careful love!'*

WOMAN ONE: and I'm running! I'm suddenly stupidly running down the road in stupid fucking shoes. Stupid I know that I felt the need to put on high heels but costume, or armour or, *yes* it feels like putting on armour and I'm *ashamed!*

ACTOR: *Ping! Ping! Ping!*

MAN ONE: My phones exploding! I get off stage buzzin', I was totally shittin' it but it went really well! Everyone's gone mad for it. Yes! That went proper alright you know, I mean I definitely ballsed up the section on the Z.M.E.T studies but I *think* I got away with it?

ACTRESS: *Ping!*

MAN ONE: Everyone's tweeting about it!

ACTRESS: *Ping! Best UX Design talk ever, feeling inspired.*

MAN ONE: Yes!

ACTRESS: *Ping! Banging keynote from the bearded manc master.*

MAN ONE: Nice.

ACTRESS: *Ping!*

MAN ONE: The videos up already?

ACTRESS: *Ping!*

MAN ONE: Oh yes, I look swish in that suit.

ACTRESS: *Ping!*

MAN ONE: Lucy Elkson, who's that? Student @NYUStern. Wow, nice photo.

LUCY: *'Enjoyed your talk today, looking forward to part two tomorrow. One question – are you ever concerned about the wellbeing of your app users?'*

ACTRESS: *Ping! Ping! Ping!*

MAN ONE: Woah, she's not very popular. Reply – '*Hello. Yes of course… How about we meet for a drink and talk about it?'*

WOMAN THREE: I've not looked at the apps all day. See? I don't need their validation to,

HACKER: *Ping!*

WOMAN THREE: Email?

HACKER: *'Send us more pics or we'll tell your family you're a slut.'*

WOMAN THREE: Must be a virus or spam or. Delete.

ACTRESS: *Ping! Ping! Ping!*

MAN ONE: People seem to like that idea.

ACTRESS: *Ping!*

MAN ONE: Tweet from Lucy.

LUCY: '*Sure, hotel bar at 7?'*

MAN ONE: Yes!

WOMAN TWO: Last time we were together yeah. I was just tryna make it work, I didn't really mean it. And like, he must've *known* I didn't mean it? We all say things we don't mean sometimes innit? Heat of the moment 'n' all that? And he *knows* me. I've been straight up from day one. Some slags got no shame, got a bare bag of bodies but pretendin' they're all prim 'n' proper cus he wants a blank canvas? Listen, if you sleep with over five men you can't expect a big wedding, you're gettin' chicken and chips love. I know that, so I'm honest from day one, fuck it. Men see sex like a sport, like exercise, and so do I. And *yes*, I've been there before, where it's *just casual* yeah, but then three months down the line you're catchin' feelings? And *nah* it gets political, that's long! So this *wasn't like that*, I *swear!* But, he is a nice fella, what can I say? And basically, yeah, we're laying together, and it was nice, and I might've sort've like. Ok fuck it, straight up. I told him I loved him. It just slipped out! *Fuck!* Urgh! I'm so fuckin' *stupid!*

WOMAN ONE: After a cry in the toilets, two sweet teas, and a very eloquent rant on Facebook, I do the presentation. But I can't concentrate, can't focus, *I can't stop fucking thinking about it!* I'm sent home early. And I cry hot snotty tears on the tube because it's not fair. I mean, I could post photos of my boyfriend online right now. But what'd be the point? Women wouldn't log on to wank over it, write nasty comments, thirty thousand. But if he did it to me? ... I just want to get home and hold him.

MAN TWO: Last night, me and the wife are/.. And it's soft at first, like we usually, soft you know, loving.

WOMAN THREE: I ignore the first one thinking it's just a joke or/.. But I get four more that day.

MAN TWO: Then out of nowhere I'm suddenly, I just want/.. I want/..

WOMAN THREE: And then mum rings, when I'm out shopping, and says she's been sent naked photos of me and she doesn't understand.

MAN TWO: I flip her over and I'm/.. And at first she's enjoying it, she seems like she's,

WOMAN THREE: And my shopping drops all over the floor, everyone turns to stare at me.

MAN TWO: I slap her arse, once, twice. I grab her hips and fuck, *hard.*

WOMAN THREE: I'm running up the road as fast as I can.

MAN TWO: She suddenly pulls away from me. She turns and, her face. The look on her face like/..

WOMAN THREE: I turn on my computer and there I am. Naked. All over the internet.

(Movement – 'shame dance' – A visceral animal reaction. Repetitive movement, squirming in shame, rabbit caught in headlights, they panic.)

WOMAN TWO: When I'm seein' someone yeah, I want his mind to be on me. So I send a little somethin', every now and then, to remind him. 'Cus there's a lot of distractions out there, let's be honest, I can't blame him for lookin'. It's shoved under his nose most of the time, some slags got no shame. And he sent me stuff all the time, look! It's not like I *miss* him, I don't even really *like* him. It was just sex, pretty good sex but yeah, just casual. I thought we both understood, no fuss, no strings. But still, he can't just cut off like that.

MAN ONE: She's waiting for me when I arrive. Her phone and a glass of red are on the table. She smiles at me, then stops herself. She's pretty, really pretty. Ok, ok, play it cool. I thank her for meeting me, order myself a glass and wait for her to begin.

LUCY: *Your twitter fans were very keen for us to meet. Should we do a selfie?*

MAN ONE: I laugh, *'sure'*. Pose. Click. Load.

LUCY: *Ping, ping, ping, ping, ping!*

MAN ONE: We turn off our phones and talk. She wants to know why I've designed an app that encourages an invasion of personal privacy. She questions my moral compass, suggests I deliberately manipulate customers. She unpicks my lecture, referencing everything I've spent the last five years studying. She's smart, and angry, and totally gorgeous. One glass down and we've relaxed a bit. Halfway through the second and I make her smile, I make her laugh. Her laugh makes my stomach flip. She touches my arm and flashes this bright white pretty smile, is she? I think she's flirting with me? She takes another sip, all red wine shy and big brown eyes and I lean in to kiss her and everything stops.

LUCY: *What are you doing?!*

MAN ONE: *'Alright darlin' don't get your knickers in a twist.'* As soon as I've said it I know it's a mistake. She's spits venom at me and storms off. Fuck. Fuuuuuuuuuck!

WOMAN ONE: My boyfriend finally comes home from work.

BOYFRIEND: *It's ok babes, I've got you.*

WOMAN ONE: He's so lovely, he strokes my hair and holds me tight.

BOYFRIEND: *I'm sure that if you speak to work and just explain everything that's been going on, I'm sure they'll understand why you got upset.*

WOMAN ONE: Upset? I'm not upset, I'm angry. There's a difference.

BOYFRIEND: *Babes, I.*

WOMAN ONE: Don't bother.

MAN ONE: I order a whiskey and check my phone. Simon and the other lecturers are in a bar down the road and do I want a beer? Not with you mate. I check her twitter, I check her Facebook. Looking through her photos I accidently hit *like* on one of them. Fuck fuck *fuck!* I laugh because it's funny, and then I stop because it's not. And then I think fuck it. I phone Simon. I'm gonna get smashed.

(MUSIC – building up in intensity.)

WOMAN THREE: I've gone viral. Is that the word? I'm all over the internet. I don't, I'm. I'm on over two hundred websites. My phone won't stop. I've been hacked, to pieces. Over and over. I can't believe this is happening.

MAN TWO: My wife rolls over and falls asleep. I watch her back breathing. I'm still hard. I take the laptop downstairs. I'm stressed and I'm tired and I've got the house to myself. And I know I probably shouldn't but, my *'probably shouldn'ts'* always lose to my *'fuck its'* every time, just one last time.

WOMAN TWO: Argh! How do you fight someone who's not there? I keep lookin' but there's nuffink, fuckin' cunt's gone, leavin' a massive nuffink. I am *sick and tired* of being told I'm not good enough. All them magazines telling me I ain't shit unless I look like that, dress like that, got a man like that? It's *embarrassin'.* Who does he fuckin' think he's messin' with? Thinks he can *ignore* me? *Me?* Thinks he can

26

just up and leave, can pick and choose like that? Fuck that, *I* do the pickin' and choosin'. *I* decide.

MAN ONE: Out with the boys, who ask no questions, but seem to somehow understand, and I don't ask about their lives, their wives, no one asks why, it's just clear we all need this night. After three shots and two pints we declare we feel alive, and look at the lights! Together we're stronger, we're soldiers, we understand. Slap on the back, fuck her man, plenty more fish and all that, don't worry mate, we'll put it right. The lads take my pain in exchange for another cold pint. 'Cus this night won't end in tears, this night we'll be loud, and lairy, and pretend we're not lonely, and do things we'll apologize for tomorrow mornin'. This night is The Night! This night is the same as every other fuckin' night but we'll do our best to pretend it isn't.

(BOOM, loud music kicks in. Chaos ensues. Each character is in their own world – MAN TWO is looking for satisfying porn. WOMAN THREE is looking at photos of herself and reading comments. WOMAN TWO is uploading pictures of her ex online and reading comments. WOMAN ONE is looking for someone to blame and reading comments about her sister. MAN ONE is drunk in a club tweeting. The two actors split the parts between them. It's loud and angry and desperate.)

WOMAN THREE: I can't stop looking at the comments. I don't want to but I find myself online.

WOMAN ONE: I find myself online. My boyfriend's fast asleep and I. I can't bear to be next to him?! I just need to fix this, there's must be some way to fix this.

MAN TWO: Scrolling through. Getting frustrated. None of this is any good. None of this is working.

WOMAN THREE: Do I look sexy yet? Is this sexy?

MAN ONE: She definitely fancied me. I was just going with the flow mate. And then she throws it back in my face?!

WOMAN THREE: My face. This first thing that comes up on Google is my face pouting and smiling.

MAN ONE: Yeah same again mate, tequila!

WOMAN TWO: Scrolling through my phone at the photos he's sent, the messages and the videos of him wanking and that.

WOMAN ONE: I can't stop thinking about it. It's driving me mad! I am so full of hate.

WOMAN TWO: And for a second yeah, I feel a bit sorry for myself, I'll admit. 'Cus we look good together.

MAN ONE: Yeah mate, she were definitely up for it. Maybe she just panicked?

WOMAN TWO: Urgh. I'm so fuckin' stupid!

MAN TWO: It's getting late, it's been twenty minutes already, I'm not hard anymore I can't.

WOMAN TWO: He can't do this to me.

MAN ONE: I can't leave it like this.

WOMAN TWO: Nah I'm not havin' it.

MAN ONE: Right. Let's sort this out.

MAN ONE: Tweet – '@LucyElkson *Red wine tipsy and I misread your signals. My mistake. Hope you enjoy the rest of the weekend.*'

MAN TWO: Click click click.

MAN ONE: *Ping!* She's replied – '*Misread?? Invented is a more appropriate verb. Publically blaming me for your inappropriate sexual advances is hardly an apology. It's another fantastic example of* @everydaysexism.' Oh fuck off.

MAN TWO: Click click click.

WOMAN THREE: Pouting and posing.

MAN ONE: Nah mate, I've got this, I'm gonna reply. Tweet – '@LucyElkson *don't be silly. The world's gone mad with political correctness. You batted your eyelids, what's a bloke supposed to think?*'

WOMAN THREE: Do I look sexy yet?

WOMAN ONE: I need to know/

WOMAN THREE: I just really need to know what they're saying about me.

WOMAN ONE: I need to know. I need to see.

MAN TWO: I need to. Fuck. I need to see/

MAN ONE: *Ping ping ping!* See! Everyone agrees with me.

WOMAN TWO: I know I shouldn't but/

MAN TWO: I know I shouldn't but/

WOMAN THREE: I know I shouldn't but/

WOMAN TWO: I put 'em on Facebook. His photos, his videos, the lot. Upload 'em to YouTube, porn sites, tag all his friends.

MAN ONE: Mate! It's all kicking off. Look at all the replies.

WOMAN TWO: Look at this fuckin' wanker, literally wankin' his small sweaty cock, look at this silly little prick. Urgh! Can't believe I even went near it.

WOMAN ONE: I can't help myself. I need to see. I know I shouldn't but, I read the comments.

WOMAN THREE: I read the comments.

WOMAN TWO: I read the comments. All my mates.

WOMAN THREE: My body.

WOMAN ONE: My baby sister.

MAN TWO: Hundreds and hundreds/

WOMAN THREE: There's thousands of them/

WOMAN ONE: Thirty thousand/

MAN TWO: Click click click/

MAN ONE: Tequila! *Ping! 'We've got your back. Stupid slut needs to be taught a lesson.'* Woah. I'm not replying to that.

WOMAN TWO: And everyone's fuckin' lovin' it, laughin' and takin' the piss.

MAN ONE: *Ping! 'Lucy Elkson can suck my dick.'* Bloody 'ell, chill out lads.

WOMAN THREE: *'Nice bod shame about the face.'*

WOMAN ONE: *'I would bang her'*

WOMAN THREE: *'She's happy to spread it'*

MAN ONE: Why'd she have to make it such a big deal? It's humiliating.

WOMAN THREE: I'm so humiliated/

WOMAN TWO: He's gonna be propa humiliated, this is fuckin' brilliant!

MAN TWO: Click click and I find one. She's younger, younger than I'd usually

WOMAN THREE: *'I'd love a go on this little one'*

MAN TWO: I'm not, I'm not like that.

MAN ONE: More shots! More shots!

MAN TWO: More girls. Younger. Firmer. Hotter. Fucking.

WOMAN ONE: *'You've got to love a slut who gets drilled in the ass'*

MAN TWO: Getting their tits out and blonde pigtails and schoolgirl skirts, and yeah bend over, and those knee high socks that are just so fucking hot.

WOMAN TWO: I don't care. I'm not 'avin' it no more, fuck that.

MAN TWO: Open it, click, and I see. She's in school uniform, there on the bed, surrounded by teddy bears.

MAN ONE: There's a fuck load of replies. Some attacking Lucy. Some attacking me.

MAN TWO: Totally gorgeous, pouting and posing for the camera, her fingers inside her knickers.

MAN ONE: Type a tweet – '@LucyElkson *No one likes a cock tease.*'

MAN TWO: Then suddenly I see it. Behind her head. A poster sellotaped to the wall.

MAN ONE: I won't actually post it, I won't actually/

MAN TWO: Pink and white. Hello Kitty. The same as Amy's. The same poster as my little girl's.

MAN ONE: Rooms spinning.

MAN TWO: I feel sick.

MAN ONE: Screens blurry. I feel sick.

WOMAN TWO: Fuck it.

MAN ONE: Fuck it. I clicked.

WOMAN TWO: Fuck it.

MAN TWO: Fucking hell. My mouth. I think a bit of sick just/

MAN ONE: I can't get her face out of my head/

MAN TWO: I can't get it out my head. That fucking cat haunts me.

WOMAN TWO: The stuff they write is brilliant, it's hilarious!

(ACTOR and ACTRESS run to centre stage and stand side by side. A movement score of individual tender loving actions – hugging, caressing face, kiss on cheek, holding hands etc – is repeated over the next section, ending in them standing still, facing us, holding hands.)

ACTOR: *'I'd tongue fuck that arse then tear it up with my cock'*

ACTRESS: *'I'd love to stick my hand up her skirt and rip down her panties and fuck the arse off her'*

ACTOR: *'I'd love to bend you over and make you scream'*

ACTRESS: *'I'll make you scream'*

ACTOR: *'I'll fucking make you scream'*

ACTRESS: *'She's perfect for any fuck, including gangbang, trust me, she can handle it'*

ACTOR: *'Stupid slut'*

ACTRESS: *'Stupid slut"*

ACTOR: *'Stupid slut likes it.'*

ACTRESS: *'Drill that bitch'*

ACTOR: *'Bang the fuck out of her'*

ACTRESS: *'I'm gonna rape that bitch'*

ACTOR: *'That's a tasty piece of pussy I'd love to fucking destroy that'*

ACTRESS: *'I'm gonna shaft that ass so hard she won't be able to sit for a month'*

ACTOR: *'I'd shove my fist up her pussy to the elbow. Her pain will be my pleasure'*

ACTRESS: *'I'm gonna brutalize that cunt so bad she'll beg me for more'*

ACTOR: *'I'm gonna rape that bitch'*

ACTRESS: *'When I'm done they'll be nothing left of her for any other man'*

ACTOR: *'Where do you want me to cum? Do you swallow?'*

ACTRESS: *'Do you like that bitch?'*

ACTOR: *'Do you like that?'*

ACTRESS: Do I look sexy? Do I? Am I sexy yet?

(Music cuts. ACTOR and ACTRESS stand still for a moment, holding hands, looking at us, they breathe. The ACTRESS is upset but pushes on to the next bit.)

WOMAN TWO: And I tell you what, it feels *fuckin' fantastic!* I don't feel bad at all, not even for a second. My mum's gone mental, said she's ashamed and it's no way to behave but I don't give a shit, I really don't. Whatever, life's short ain't it? Gotta look after yourself in this world 'cus ain't no one gonna do it for ya. He's got loads of photos of me he could use. But he ain't. He's still silent. Must have been deletin' 'em, fuckin' mug. Lucky really. So now he's done what he's done, humiliated me like that, so I shamed him. And now everyone knows what he is, and the next fella I'm with will know not to fuck about. It's a win win.

Tell you what, they weren't lyin' when they said revenge is sweet. It's sugar-coated.

(Beat. The ACTOR asks if the ACTRESS is ok. They check in with each other, it's kind and loving and honest. Silence. WOMAN THREE's light flashes on interrupting the joy. Both actors look at the light, neither of them wants to do the next bit. The light is persistent. The ACTRESS takes a deep breath and walks to stand under the light.)

WOMAN THREE: I've not left the house in days. I know where my edges are, and all of them ache. They have no right to see my body, I didn't give them permission to do that, the photos weren't for them, they were for me. I start to wonder if all men are like this. Do all men think like that about women? And it's just that some make the choice to be polite, to be kind? I wonder if they've got mothers, or sisters, or girlfriends. Women who really love them, who have no idea? I wonder how they walk down the street, how they get through their day with all those horrible thoughts about the women around them. I wonder how they don't go mad with all that hate.

MAN ONE: Guilt wakes me in the morning. Guilt is in my mouth, lying thick and fuzzy on my teeth. All my organs feel dirty. I'm a bit too scared to move actually in case something breaks so I'm keeping very still. My heart is beating very fast. Too fucking fast, it shouldn't be beating this fast it's never done this before I think I'm dying and ok, ok it's ok you're ok, you're ok, ok roll over slowly and she's there. Shiny. Her light pulsing, laughing at me. No. No no no no no open it and check and yes, oh fuck, oh my fuck, I need to be sick.

WOMAN ONE: What do you watch? When no one's looking what do you/.. Do they look like me? Are they blonde? Should I dye my, I could dye my, I could if you wanted it's no/... Their boobs bigger than mine? Bet they are. Are they fake? Do you like that, do you wish mine were like that? Do you think of 'em when you're/.. Do you think of them when we're/... Do they do things I don't do? Is that

why you, do they do anal? I bet they do, do you like that,
do you wish I did that? I could do that. I could. If I wanted
to, if you, wanted, if I… Do they dress up? Schoolgirls?
Want me to? What do you watch can I see, can I see what
you watch?

BOYFRIEND: *Stop.*

WOMAN ONE: He says,

BOYFRIEND: *Stop.*

WOMAN ONE: I can't.

BOYFRIEND: *Stop.*

WOMAN ONE: I can't stop looking. I need to/.. Oh god.
Have you seen it? Who showed you, some bloke down
the pub? My baby sister, did you like it? Did you think of
me, compare me to

BOYFRIEND: *Stop.*

WOMAN ONE: Stop.

BOYFRIEND: *Stop.*

WOMAN ONE: I can't.

BOYFRIEND: *Stop.*

WOMAN ONE: I can't.

MAN ONE: I swipe through the carnage. I've committed social
suicide and Lucy's getting rape threats. What am I going to
do? Dave's text me six times, he's read the tweets and,

DAVE: It's totally inappropriate, I'm doing my best to smooth
it over but *what the fuck?*

MAN ONE: My sister's emailed from home, she's seen it
and thinks I've gone barmy,

SISTER: *That poor young girl!*

MAN ONE: I've got a missed call from Frank at *Bright Young
Minds,* fuck fuck fuck! How am I going to get through
today? I've got to shower, and put on a suit, and drink a
coffee and go give a lecture. Three thousand students. I've
got to speak words, that make sense, to three thousand
students and a live Twitter feed. All of which will want an
explanation, there must be an explanation surely? How
am I going to get through today? My heart is thumping so
fucking, I'm not going to make it, it's too far.

HACKER: *Ping!*

MAN ONE: There's another one. Emails from strangers telling me they've got my back. They've launched a DDoS Attack on *Bright Young Minds* and won't remove it until she's kicked off the course. This is ridiculous! Surely they can't, Dave rings.

DAVE: *'Lucy's gone.'*

MAN ONE: What?!

DAVE: *'She's gone. Just don't fuck up the lecture today and it'll all blow over.'*

MAN ONE: Fuckin' ell.

(Beat.)

WOMAN TWO: Everyone's going mad about it. My so-called mates sayin' shit like what I done was bang out of order, proper lowest of the low stuff. The girls at work are callin' me a stupid bitch, and a 'spurned woman', which no one even says anymore like *what?* Tracey reckons HR have heard and they're probly gonna suspend me, 'til it all blows over. So much for sisterhood eh? You're meant to have my back on this girls! The blokes ain't sayin' shit, it's the women kickin' off! Mum's really upset, says she's *mortified.* And yeah that ain't nice but it's done now ain't it, what am I meant to do? Whatever, I'm proud of what I done. I stood up for myself. Fuckin' idiots.

WOMAN THREE: I got recognized in the street. Waiting for the seventy-two, that takes me home past the shops, I look up and this man's staring at me. And for half a second, for half a second I really think maybe he fancies me. And then I realize. He gets his phone out, looks at it, looks at me, looks at it looks at me and smiles. I watch his mouth smile and I feel sick.

MAN TWO: I've stopped watching it. It's been a whole week! I've started jogging, I'm choosing jogging over wanking, I've signed up for the London Marathon… *Fuck.* Breathe. … I can't concentrate, can't focus.

WOMAN THREE: The bus comes and I jump on it, and I'm blinking back tears so I might be wrong here, but I think he took a photo of me through the window. I think about dying. Not in a dramatic way. I just consider it. And how much easier that'd be, for everyone, a nice chapter ending, quiet and simple.

MAN TWO: Then at work Susan calls an urgent meeting to announce the company's making redundancies. And there's nothing we can do but wait. I get home to bills and mess and Spaghetti fucking bolognaise *again*, and we're at the dinner table when Amy suddenly announces she's got a boyfriend. I can't eat. My wife asks me what's wrong and/.. I tell her I'm fine. She'd prefer me to lie, honestly. She begs me to open up, but the truth is most women can't stomach it. They want us to keep pretending… I took the poster down. I couldn't look at it anymore and/.. Amy's upset, she doesn't understand what she did wrong. *It's not that darling, it's not that it's/..*

WOMAN THREE: I consented when I took the photos, it's my fault.

MAN TWO: *It's not your fault. It has nothing to do with you.*

WOMAN THREE: It's all anonymous online. There's no culpability, there's no one to blame, except the person in the photo. So it must be my fault.

MAN ONE: No business class for me on the flight back. Squished up between two sweaty suits on their phones. Clicks and swipes, clicks and swipes. Economy's always felt more like home anyway to be honest. Day two at *Bright Young Minds* was hell on earth. Second lecture done, hungover to fuck, to three thousand angry faces. Holding my breath, waiting for someone to say something, why didn't anyone say something? Lucy got rape threats, death threats. I got a slap on the wrist and whipped out of there quick, come on big lad, taxi to the airport, off you go. Doesn't make sense. My sister phoned, she's gonna pick me up from the airport, drive me home. I can't wait to be honest, get out of the spotlight, get out of this suit. I messaged Lucy, said I'd like to apologise, left my number. She hasn't called. I hope one day she does, I owe her at least that.

WOMAN TWO: I got suspended from work. Fucksake! Why couldn't I just let it go? Now everyone hates me, what am I gonna do? Worst part is, he ain't even replied, *nothin'*. After all that he's still winnin'? Must have seen it and just decided to stay *silent?* It's fuckin' killin' me. I need him to say somethin' to do *somethin'*. I thought I was gonna feel better.

MAN TWO: I leave them at the dinner table, tell my wife I'm fine, I'm fine I'm going for a drive. But I just sit in the car. I sit there and/.. *I just, need, quiet!* ... Fuck. Breathe... This car's a mess. It's disgusting, I'm going to have to, how does it get so disgusting so quickly it's, wrappers and toys and shit everywhere and. That's when I spot it. Scrunched up and stuffed down the side of the seat. Amy's sweaty Sex-Ed leaflets, hidden. *'talking together, about sex and relationships... everything you need to know about contraception...puberty, relationships and sex, talking to your children with confidence.'* Fuck. She's hiding them? That's what I've taught her? Embarrassed my daughter into hiding. That's the kind of father I am? They should write one for us, eh? *'how not to fuck up your kids...how to be a good dad.'* Oh bloody hell. Maybe I could just stay in this car forever.

(Movement – we see the actors and they see us. An exhale. Repetitive score of abstract movements as seen before.)

WOMAN ONE: My sisters in hospital. Overdose. They're thinking it was an accident but/.. I mean she's just eighteen, looking at me and I haven't got a clue. I mean, no one taught *me*. I used to sneak glances at page three to check if I looked like that. I watched her do the same as me, technology speeding it all up. Touch screens teaching us to fuck before we're learning to touch. She's always on her phone, and I didn't stop it. I didn't stop it. She's on well over two hundred websites, more and more men are clicking. Every time I check the number is bigger. And by checking, I'm actually increasing the view count, so every time I look I'm making it worse. But I need to look, I can't stop looking, I need to see.

MAN TWO: There was this girl once. Sarah. Phwoar. She was./
… Stunning, fucking *stunning*. We were in the same class
at Uni, and one night at this party she comes up to me,
completely out of the blue. I mean I'd seen her, of course
I had, everyone had seen Sarah, but we'd never spoken.
I mean she was so out of my league, so out of everyone's
league, Sarah was in her own fucking league. Sarah was
Cristiano Ronaldo, and I was some fat old bloke paying for
some shitty pub team. But here she was? I couldn't fucking
believe it.

And it was, great. Kissing her was like/.. Electric. I mean,
she was *so fucking hot*, and she's letting me touch her?
She's letting me take her bra off? She's letting me, oh
fuck, *yeeeees*!! And then somehow, right at a really crucial
moment, I go soft. Fuck. *Fuuuuck! I don't know what's
happening, this never happens I'm sorry I, you're so beautiful
and, maybe it's the beer or, fuck, fuck, FUCK!* And she gets
really annoyed, which is kind of understandable, and I
get really embarrassed and it's so awful it's, I want to die.
Really I, I mean dying is definitely preferable to both of us
staring at my cock wondering why it's suddenly decided to
stop working. And she trying, bless her she's trying. She's
tugging on it and sucking on it, asking if it's her and *fuck
no, no! It's not you it's, I, it's. That's just making it worse babe,*
when it couldn't really get much worse and. She left. Never
spoke to me again. Beautiful girls are cruel man. I love my
wife. I love my children, I'm happy. But porn is/.. It fills a
gap, everyone's got a gap, right? Five clicks gives you five
minutes of what you think you want and you don't even
have to speak to them, don't have to risk/.. Sex is terrifying
for men. *(Beat.)* I feel sick with it, urgh, guilt eats you up
doesn't it, that proper guilt, you know?

WOMAN ONE: My sister's awake. The bed makes her look so
tiny. Hospitals stink, I try to open the window, *get some fresh
air, have they locked this fucking?!* She stops me. I look at her
and it all comes out. *I'm sorry, I'm so sorry, I'm meant to be the
big sister, I'm.* She stops me. She takes my hand and pulls
me down to lay with her. We lay together.

WOMAN THREE: I'm laying on the floor, staring at the walls, singing into the carpet. For some reason I've had *all things bright and beautiful* in my head for days now. *(Hums a bit.)* I think about tracing around my hand with crayons at school. Chasing shadows across the playground. And somehow there on the carpet something somewhere inside me cracks, and I sit up. I can't explain I/.. I just/.. Surely there must be something in between invisible and everywhere? I've got lost, yes, spilled out of my skin, over the edges and, I want a reclaiming somehow. This is my body, the edges blurred but, it is mine.

WOMAN TWO: I deleted 'em. And I wrote this big long sorry message on my wall, took me ages to write it, pick the right words and that. It's a bit soppy but fuck it, it's honest. Mum said well done, said it takes a strong woman to admit it when she's wrong, and I reckon she's right. I wrote him a letter too. I can't send it, obviously, cus he's still fuckin' disappeared but I read it out in the park and I burnt it. I know that's a bit mad but d'you know what, it was like doing that yeah, felt really good, felt like I was forgivin' myself. Everyone makes mistakes. I've come off Facebook and that. And I'm not seein' anyone at the moment, havin' a little break. Life's too short for all that drama, trust me, I don't *miss it at all.* I've started doin' yoga down the gym. It's amazin'. I feel propa spiritual, really connected. And the instructor is well fit.

WOMAN THREE: I went online this morning, for the first time I mean, since it all/.. I hadn't looked at the photos in ages, I'd only read the comments. But this morning I looked at them, looked at me. My photos. My body. And I felt/.. I look/.. I look like me.

MAN TWO: I put the poster back up. Amy's pleased. I've been following Susan's new policy at work and so far so good. Me and the missus have been spending more time together and it's/.. It is what it is.

WOMAN ONE: My sister's home. There's therapy and pills and, I don't know. Some things can't be cured with pills but, there's hope… I don't even blame him. He's a fucking idiot but he's, just *young,* just young… I don't know where we go from here? I don't know what we do now?

WWW.OBERONBOOKS.COM